FIRST PEOPLES

INUIT

VALERIE BODDEN

CREATIVE EDUCATION · CREATIVE PAPERBACKS

Published by Creative Education and Creative Paperbacks
P.O. Box 227, Mankato, Minnesota 56002
Creative Education and Creative Paperbacks are imprints of
The Creative Company
www.thecreativecompany.us

Design by Christine Vanderbeek
Production by Colin O'Dea
Art direction by Rita Marshall
Printed in the United States of America

Photographs by Alamy (Albert Knapp, robertharding, Science
History Images), Creative Commons Wikimedia (A.P. Fot.,
Goetze, Seattle, Wash./Library of Congress; Edward S.
Curtis/Library of Congress Prints & Photographs Division;
Lomen Bros./Library of Congress; Antonion Zeno Shindler/
Smithsonian American Art Museum; U.S. National Archives
and Records Administration), Getty Images (Thomas J.
Abercrombie/National Geographic, Yvette Cardozo, ull-
stein bild Dtl., Gordon Wiltsie), iStockphoto (mscornelius),
Shutterstock (Miloje, Emre Tarimcioglu, Antero Topp)

Library of Congress Cataloging-in-Publication Data
Names: Bodden, Valerie, author.
Title: Inuit / Valerie Bodden.
Series: First peoples.
Includes bibliographical references and index.
Summary: An introduction to the Inuit lifestyle and history,
including their forced relocation and how they keep tradi-
tions alive today. An Inuit story recounts how the northern
lights came to exist.
Identifiers:
ISBN 978-1-64026-226-3 (hardcover)
ISBN 978-1-62832-789-2 (pbk)
ISBN 978-1-64000-361-3 (eBook)
This title has been submitted for CIP processing under LCCN
2019938367.
CCSS: RI.1.1, 2, 3, 4, 5, 6, 7; RI.2.1, 2, 3, 4, 5, 6; RI.3.1, 2, 3, 5;
RF.1.1, 3, 4; RF.2.3, 4

First Edition HC   9 8 7 6 5 4 3 2 1
First Edition PBK   9 8 7 6 5 4 3 2 1

FIRST PEOPLES

TABLE *of* CONTENTS

ARCTIC PEOPLE

The Inuit lived in the ARCTIC. Many Inuit lived near the Atlantic, Pacific, or Arctic Oceans. Others lived farther away from the sea.

 Today's Inuit are known as Alaska Inuit, Central Inuit (Canada), and Greenland Inuit.

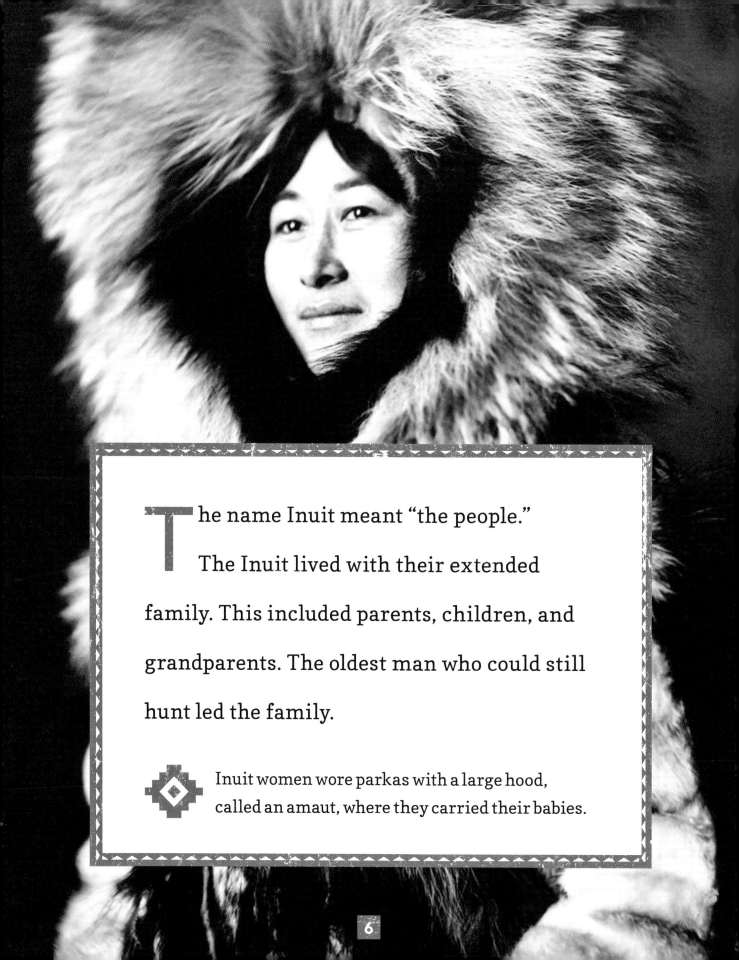

The name Inuit meant "the people." The Inuit lived with their extended family. This included parents, children, and grandparents. The oldest man who could still hunt led the family.

Inuit women wore parkas with a large hood, called an amaut, where they carried their babies.

INUIT LIFE

Most Inuit lived in homes called karmats. These homes were dug into the ground. The walls were made of stones or logs. A few Inuit groups built igloos. They stayed in the igloos during winter hunts.

 Water-resistant sealskin and caribou fur are still used to make mukluks, or boots.

Inuit men hunted seals and whales with HARPOONS. Some hunted caribou with bows and arrows. Many Inuit fished, too. Women prepared the food. They melted ice to get drinking water.

 The Inuit used every part of the animals they hunted to make clothing, tents, tools, and more.

On land, the Inuit traveled on wooden sleds. The sleds were pulled by dogs or people. The Inuit built boats to get around at sea.

Sled dogs also sniffed out seals and warned of threats such as polar bears.

SPIRITUAL CEREMONIES

The Inuit believed that everything had a spirit. They held CEREMONIES to keep the spirits happy. Men wore masks for some ceremonies.

 Masks were carved from wood or whalebone, and drums were made from animal skins.

TRADING FURS AND HUNTING WHALES

In the 1700s, many fur traders came to the Arctic. Whale hunters arrived in the mid-1800s. Some Inuit got jobs on the whaling ships.

 Working for whalers meant the Inuit had less time for hunting and other activities.

In the 1940s, the government set up schools for Inuit children. Students were not allowed to speak their own language. In some places, Inuit families were forced to move.

 In public schools far from home, Inuit children were not allowed to wear their fur clothing.

BEING INUIT

Today, most Inuit still live in or near the Arctic. Many live in cities. They travel by snowmobiles instead of sleds. But they still hold ceremonies. They study the Inuit language. They try to keep their TRADITIONS alive.

 The Inuit are known for being kind and giving, which are valuable qualities among the people.

AN INUIT STORY

The Inuit told stories to pass the long winters. In one, Wolverine stole the moon and the sun. A boy told his village that he would get the sun and the moon back. The boy made Wolverine sweep the moonlight and sunlight out of his home. Snow was mixed in with the light. The boy made snowballs. He threw them into the sky. The snowballs burst into moving lights. These became the NORTHERN LIGHTS.

GLOSSARY

ARCTIC ➤ the part of the world that is farthest north

CEREMONIES ➤ special acts carried out according to set rules

HARPOONS ➤ spears attached to ropes and used for hunting large sea animals

NORTHERN LIGHTS ➤ moving lights that sometimes fill the sky in the Arctic

TRADITIONS ➤ beliefs, stories, or ways of doing things that are passed down from parents to their children

READ MORE

Fullman, Joe. *Native North Americans: Dress, Eat, Write, and Play Just Like the Native Americans.* Mankato, Minn.: QEB, 2010.

Morris, Ting. *Arts and Crafts of the Native Americans.* North Mankato, Minn.: Smart Apple Media, 2007.

WEBSITES

Inuit Cultural Online Resource
https://www.icor.ottawainuitchildrens.com/
Check out videos and photos of present-day Inuit.

Inuulitsivik: Northern Life and Inuit Culture
http://www.inuulitsivik.ca/northern-life-and-inuit-culture
Learn more about Inuit life today.

Note: Every effort has been made to ensure that the websites listed above are suitable for children, that they have educational value, and that they contain no inappropriate material. However, because of the nature of the Internet, it is impossible to guarantee that these sites will remain active indefinitely or that their contents will not be altered.

INDEX